Born To Win

Feridon E. Terry, Sr., MBA

Terry's Media Magic

feridon@feridonterry.com

ISBN-10: **1490452834**

ISBN-13: **978-1490452838**

"A Feridon Terry Book"

First Print 2016

Printed in USA

Edited by: Gina Powell

All quoted scripture in this book are from the King James Bible.

Born to Win

DEDICATION

This book is dedicated to my family. My wife Joy, daughter Kayla, and my son Feridon Terry, Jr., I love you all. To my parents thank you for continuing to encourage and believe in me. Rest in peace,

Grandma Annie Johnson

FORWARD

My grandmother, Annie M. Allen Johnson taught me the importance of obtaining an education. She made it clear that what I learned could not be taken away from me. She talked to me about how to be a wife. She shared skills that she learned in the kitchen, in the workplace and in the family. She loved others by sharing words of wisdom and serving them. I love you, grandma.

Grandma, you live in my mom, uncle, aunt, brother, sister and my children. Your legacy continues in my cousins, nieces, and nephews. Grandma you taught me that in life it is important to trust God. Your legacy of teaching and loving others is in me.

With Love Your Granddaughter,

Joy Shirelle Drumgold Terry, Psy.D., LCP

TABLE OF CONTENTS

Acknowledgments

Chapters

1   Courage

2   Fail Harder

3   Surround Yourself With the Right People

4   Financial Literacy 101

5   The Truth About Debt

6   Entrepreneurship

7   The Power of the Mind

8   Vision

9   An Effective Leader

10 Train Up Your Children

11 Born to Win

ACKNOWLEDGMENTS

Thank you Lord, for all you have done for me. My parents were my first teachers. The many lessons on life and the examples in which they have provided for me are priceless. My father was my 4th, 5th and 6th grade teacher. As a young boy that was difficult to handle, with all the peer pressure in regards to being the teacher's son. Before he was my teacher, I was a C student at best. Afterwards, I was able to maintain honor roll all the way through high school. I was able to maintain a 3.1 GPA in college and a 3.64 GPA in graduate school. He had no time for a lazy son, he instilled hard work ethics in my mind. While growing up mother was my motivator. She always believed in my abilities as student and the many talents that I possessed. She always said that I could be whatever I wanted to be. I believed that growing up as a kid. She didn't believe in doing things in a half manner. She taught me to give everything that I am doing my very best. My mother and father are firm believers in doing what is right. Even when it is not popular among people, do what's right anyway. My fathers' words were, "if you are doing what's right I can defend you, but if you are doing wrong I cannot defend you" and he stood firm on that.

My grandfather taught me at the young age of 3 years old how to work hard at your own business and dreams. He owned an ice cream truck in Queens, New York. I used to ride with him and remember the kids chasing the sound of the truck down the street until he stopped. My sister used to handle the money while my grandfather handed out the ice cream. At the end of each day, he wanted his inventory of ice cream, snacks, gum, etc. completely empty. "Have something of your own," is what he told me all of my life, when I would sit down and have conversations with him.

I AM

Born to Win

1 COURAGE

Joshua 1:9 "Have I not commanded you? Be strong and courageous. Do not be frightened, and do not be dismayed, for the Lord your God is with you wherever you go."

What is Courage? Dictionary.com defines courage to be the quality of mind or spirit that enables a person to face difficulty, danger, pain, etc., without fear. Fear has devoured so many dreams. What is it about fear that will make one so uneasy about their situation? Most people fear failure only because that's what they have been taught, especially in school. Nobody wants to be a failure. Failure is only an opportunity to improve in areas where we struggle. This is where courage steps in. You are going to have some ups and down. Most people give up on themselves when faced with difficult obstacles. The true challenge of growth comes when you have set backs. It takes courage to start all over again. It takes courage to say, I will not let this hold me down. When you have that hunger to succeed, the courage that you possess within will help you to seek what it is you hunger for. With courage, you must accept full responsibility of what takes place in your life.

That way you will not waste time blaming or pointing fingers at others about how your life has turned out. Your focus has to stay on the light ahead of you. That's why some people are not where they are supposed to be in life because they spend most of their time blaming others. Own up to what has happened so that you can keep moving forward. Take responsibility and believe that you will take yourself where you want to go.

Deuteronomy 31:6 "Be strong and courageous. Do not be afraid or terrified because of them, for the Lord your God goes with you, he will never leave you nor forsake you." The word of God says, be strong and courageous. The three Hebrew boys Shadrach, Meshach and Abednego demonstrated strength and courage. Daniel 3: They were determined not to worship King Nebuchadnezzar's gods nor his image that he created. "If we are thrown into the blazing furnace, the God we serve is able to deliver us from it, and he will deliver us from Your Majesty's hand. But even if he does not, we want you to know, Your Majesty, that we will not serve your gods or worship the image of gold you have set up."

King Nebuchadnezzar was upset by this and heated the fiery furnace 7 times more than what it normally was. It was so hot that the flames from it killed the guards who threw them in. Then Nebuchadnezzar the king was astonished, and rose up in haste, and spake, and said unto his counsellors, "Did not we cast three men bound into the midst of the fire? They answered and said unto the king, True, O king. He answered and said, Lo, I see four men loose, walking in the midst of the fire, and they have no hurt; and the form of the fourth is like the Son of God!" Courage will have you to stand on what you believe. It will have you stare the lion in its face and say, "I am not afraid." When you have that courage to take a stand, God will take care of the rest.

The story of David and Goliath is found in 1 Samuel 17. Where a young man who was just a little older than a boy had the courage to stand against this fearsome giant Goliath. All the other Israelites feared the Philistine giant. Young David knew that with the Lord on his side, there was nothing that could stop him. He ran to face Goliath. He slung a smooth rock that hit the champion Goliath in the forehead and killed him. When things get difficult it is not time to get scared or give in. When you look up the word difficult on Google it means needing much effort or skill to accomplish, deal with, or understand. In order to deal with difficult situations you have to switch gears. We all have to face difficult situations. Young David took action, he switched gears and did what everyone else was scared to do. "These things I have spoken unto you, that in me ye might have peace. In the world ye shall have tribulation: but be of good cheer; I have overcome the world". John 16:33. In the midst of it all, whatever you are faced with, you have to stand on courage. You will be faced with obstacles that will almost seem impossible to conquer but you were designed in such a way, with the help of God, to conquer anything. I was fortunate enough to grow up with two positive and courageous men in my father and grandfather. I looked at these men who taught me a lot by example. It was hard to grasp the understanding of what my father meant by, "life will happen but you can't let it get you down, you can't let people get you out of your character, find a way." As a young man, that was hard to rationalize. It was hard to understand that meaning. I have never witnessed these two men in my life be bothered by anything. I didn't understand it. They were not bothered because they knew and understood that no matter what, God will make a way. When you are courageous and have that type of mentality, it brushes off onto your family. When you have been through the fire and still have courage, that is courage under fire.

I came to a point in my life where I had to understand that being afraid to take chances was just going to land me in the same position that I was in. Isaiah 41: 10; "So do not fear, for I am with you; do not be dismayed, for I am your God. I will strengthen you and help you; I will up hold you with my righteous right hand." I had no reason to fear anything but every reason to trust God. When I learned how to trust God that is when I started having success. Fear is just a figment of our imaginations. We fool ourselves out with nothing. Although, you are in the fire, you can still see your way out. Courage, stand on it, believe, and stay strong.

Chapter 1 Reflections

What did you learn about courage?

_____

_____

_____

_____

_____

_____

_____

_____

_____

_____

_____

_____

_____

"I learned that courage was not the absence of fear, but the triumph

over it. The brave man is not he who does not feel afraid, but he

who conquers that fear." – Nelson Mandela

2 Fail Harder

Philippians 4:13 "I can do all things through him who strengthens me."

Most of us were taught that failing was bad. Nobody wants to fail but do not be afraid to fail. Many lessons are taught through failure. It is an opportunity to work on your weaknesses, an opportunity to grow stronger.

I am a fan of sports. Let me share an illustrative story about two guys who were playing basketball. After they finish shooting around one guy says, "I did not miss any of my free throws today." The other guy replied, "how many did you shoot?" He said, "15". The guy replied. "I shot 100 free throws today and missed 15." One guy shot 85 more free throws than his peer. He was willing to fail harder. He missed as many as his peer made. In the end he will have more success because he was willing to go the extra mile.

Do not be afraid to make decisions. You cannot be afraid to fail because you will be scared to make the necessary steps towards your destiny. When you fail, and feel down and out, what reason can you think of or remember to help you get back up? Stop running from your pain, because your pain and your struggle is what you should use to drive you. Recall how God brought you through a difficult time in your life. He did not leave you then and he has not left you now. When you reach that goal that seemed to be plagued with failure it will be that much sweeter because you know what you had to go through to get there. If you are serious, you would go all out and not worry about the hiccups that may occur.

Failure is just temporary but will be permanent if you quit. "There hath no temptation taken you but such as is common to man: but God is faithful, who will not suffer you to be tempted above that ye are able; but will with the temptation also make a way to escape, that ye may be able to bear it", I Corinthians10:13. It may seem like it is over. It may seem like it is too much to bare. It may seem like it is impossible because what you have to endure but God will never put more on you than you can bare. It doesn't take any effort to be a loser. It will take everything in you to be a winner or a champion because of who you are. Our genetic makeup is already setup up for us to win. And God said, "Let us make man in our image, after our likeness: and let them have dominion over the fish of the sea, and over the fowl of the air, and over the cattle, and over all the earth, and over every creeping thing that creepeth upon the earth". Genesis 1:26. We are made up in God's image and after his likeness. This scripture speaks volumes. Think about it for second, and then think about who God is. He is King of Kings and Lord of Lords, by definition "we" his children are of royalty. By definition WE ARE BORN TO WIN! With that notion you have to realize that no matter what happens in life, you are still destined to win. If you quit because you have a few bumps in the road or a couple of setbacks then you have given into the realm of defeat. There is no success without some type of challenge, struggle or failure.

Notable people who have failed but yet succeeded:

Thomas Edison- teachers said he was "too stupid to learn anything." He was fired from his first two jobs for being "non-productive." As an inventor, Edison made 1,000 unsuccessful attempts at inventing the light bulb. When a reporter asked, "How did it feel to fail 1,000 times?" Edison replied, "I didn't fail 1,000 times. The light bulb was an invention with 1,000 steps."

Michael Jordan - I've missed more than 9000 shots in my career. I've lost almost 300 games. 26 times I've been trusted to take the game winning shot and missed. I've failed over and over again in my life. That is why I succeed."

Vera Wang - failed to make the U.S. Olympic figure-skating team. Then she became an editor at Vogue and was passed over for the editor-in-chief position.

Theodore Seuss Geisel, aka Dr. Seuss - had his first book rejected by 27 different publishers.

Walt Disney - Was fired by a newspaper editor because he "lacked imagination and had no good ideas." He started a number of businesses that didn't last long and eventually went bankrupt before he started Disneyland.

There are many more people who have failed over and over

but the key is they never gave up or gave in. If you have failed one time or a hundred times, what is it all worth to you? If you quit, it didn't mean much. If it means everything to you, then you will find a way. Each of these individuals learned something each time they have failed. They built on what didn't work. They didn't let failing hinder them from where it was they were trying to go. Imagine if Thomas Edison had given up, we could possibly be sitting in the dark. A man who has failed 1000 times, but yet he kept his eyes on the end result. That's what you have to do, focus on the end result. You have to change your perspective about failing and use it to your advantage. With struggle comes success.

Do not be afraid to take risks. Playing it safe will keep you in your current situation. Many people fail to realize that there are risks involved with anything that you do. A dream will be just a dream if you don't devise a plan and execute it. You will find yourself dreaming the rest of your life. You will be thinking and having those "what if" thoughts. When you drive a car you are taking a risk. The reason it seems like nothing to you is because you have developed confidence in your driving abilities. The more you drive the more practice you have received. You need to develop that same confidence in your abilities to achieve your dreams.

Chapter 2 Reflections

Now that you know that look at failure from a different perspective, how will you now go forward when failure happens to you?

_____

_____

_____

_____

_____

_____

_____

_____

_____

_____

_____

_____

_____

_____

_____

_____

_____

_____

_____

_____

_____

_____

_____

_____

Did you know?

Sidney Poitier: After his first audition, Poitier was told by the casting director, "Why don't you stop wasting people's time and go out and become a dishwasher or something?" Poitier vowed to become one of the most well-regarded actors in the business.

3 Surround Yourself With The Right People

Proverbs 13:20 "Whoever walks with the wise becomes wise, but the companion of fools will suffer harm."

To be successful, you must surround yourself with the right people. Be sure to surround yourself with people who are smarter than you. They will bring you brilliant ideas that you can add with your own.

Another way to be successful is to associate yourself with positive people. They will find positive things in bad or negative situations. Negative people are not good to have around you. They will not find anything positive in whatever you are doing. They will always come up with a reason or reasons why something will not work. They will complain and be a nuisance to your circle. Negative people will start making you see things negative. You won't even notice that everything you say and do will start to become negative. 1 Corinthians 15:33 "Be not deceived: evil communications corrupt good manners."

You don't necessarily want haters in your circle but do not be afraid of them. Haters are just secret admirers. They are just people who envy what you are doing and what you have. The ideas that you have developed, haters will not like them because they did not think of them first. Haters can be used as measuring tools. Use them to measure your success. The more success that you have, the more haters you will obtain. Don't just view haters in a negative spectrum, yet use them to motivate you to accomplish your goals and ideas.

You cannot be successful if people with a "pond water" mentality are surrounding you. You have to have people who have that river flow mentality around you. The reason being is rivers lead to oceans. In order to be successful you have to have forward thinking. Your people on your team have to be forward thinkers. If you can think forward, then you will make forward progress towards your goals. Backwards thinking will have you going in the opposite direction of where you are trying to go.

What does this means for your friends? If your friends are not encouraging you to do great things, they are not your friends. If they are becoming a stumbling block to you, then you will have to make a decision of whether or not you want to keep that friend who is keeping you from achieving your goals and dreams. A true friend will step aside so that you can do what you have to do. Your friends must be forward thinkers as well. If you are a forward thinker and your friends think backwards, you will find yourself stuck in between.

Whatever you are set out to do, you have to be around people who are already doing what you want to do, or have that same mentality as you. If you want to become a millionaire you cannot surround yourself with people who are broke or have a broke mindset. You have to connect with people with a million dollar mindset or people who have millions. It is not hard to do. You must first listen to the way people talk. Watch their actions and then you will know if they are a fit for you.

Notice when you post something on social media about a job that you recently received, you will get 283 likes and 83 comments. However, if you post something on social media about you starting a business, you will get 6 likes and 3 comments. When you tell the people you know that you have started a business, they are afraid you will ask them for their support.

Your success should not make anyone around you feel uneasy. If it does, you need to reevaluate your circle.

Chapter 3 Reflections

Now you know that it is important to have the right people surrounding you. How will you go forward to ensure the right people are surrounding you?

_____

_____

_____

_____

_____

_____

_____

_____

_____

_____

_____

_____

_____

_____

_____

_____

_____

_____

_____

_____

_____

_____

_____

_____

_____

_____

_____

_____

_____

"Surround yourself with only people who are going to lift you

higher." – Oprah Winfrey

4 Financial Literacy 101

2 Corinthians 9:8 "And God is able to make all grace abound toward you; that ye, always having all sufficiency in all things, may abound to every good work."

Financial Literacy is so important. It is something that is not necessarily stressed in school systems but it needs to be. Proverbs 22:7 "The rich ruleth over the poor, and the borrower *is* servant to the lender." According to the Federal Reserve the amount of revolving credit card debt is 882 billion dollars as of May 2015. 35 percent of Americans have unpaid bills that are reported to collection agencies according to the Huffington Post as of August 7, 2015. 40 million Americans have at least one student loan debt according to CNN as of September 2014. What this translates to is that many people spend their lives in financial slavery. They are slaving trying to pay back their debts.

The "60/40 Rule" - this is a simple budgetary rule to live by. Luke 14:28 states "for which of you, intending to build a tower, sitteth not down first, and counteth the cost, whether he have *sufficient* to finish *it*?" Even Jesus knows that counting the cost or knowing how to budget your money is important. A budget will help you to avoid spending money that you do not have. It will also help you to save, invest and have play money. Simply by living on 60 percent of your income you allow the other 40 percent to invest in yourself. The 60 percent is all your bills that you have to pay. This is your mortgage/rent, car note etc. The 40 percent is broken down into a few categories; Tithes, freedom investing, long term saving, emergency and play. You take these out each time you receive money, salaries, etc. Open four savings accounts and direct your funds to the freedom investing account, long term savings account, emergency fund account, and play money account.

I am a witness and a firm believer in giving tithes and offerings. Malachi 3:10 Bring ye all the tithes into the storehouse, that there may be meat in mine house, and prove me now herewith, saith the LORD of hosts, if I will not open you the windows of heaven, and pour you out a blessing, that there shall not be room enough to receive it. Since I have been doing so, I have had to give some of my blessings away to others because it was so much. The percent that you want to give is 10%.

Your freedom investing should be for just that, FREEDOM. This account is going to help you to be free from financial slavery. This is what you are going to use for investing in a business, real estate, etc. The amount that needs to be allocated for this is 10%. This account is designed to help you earn money. You want to have multiple streams of income.

Your long term savings account is used for your vacations, upgrades to your home, or whatever you need to save for. The amount of funds that needs to be allocated to this account is 10%. "Many people don't plan to fail but they fail to plan" -John L. Beckley. This quote is true because people will jump up and decide to go on a vacation or buy something that they did not plan for, spend all of their money and come back home broke. You have to count the cost. Do your research. If a trip to Vegas costs $3000, this account (depending on your salary) will not only pay for the trip but you will have some spending money along with it in a years' time.

The emergency fund account is just what it is for, emergencies. Anything can happen at any given moment. Your tire could blow out, car repairs, house repair etc. The amount that you need to allocate to this fund is 5%.

Everybody needs to have play money. This is the money that you use to go out on a date, or buy something that you may not necessarily need but you want it. This is the money that you have fun with. You should allocate 5% to this account.

This system is designed to keep you from getting in a bunch of debt. When you have solid system such as this one. You can win in the financial arena of your life.

An issue in America is that schools will prepare you to be employees but very few will prepare you to be financially responsible. Yet we still cannot use this an excuse to be irresponsible when it comes to finances. For one, the bible has many scriptures regarding finances and we need to pay close attention to them. There are many financial resources that we can use, some of which will be shared later. The next few paragraphs will have scriptures regarding finances and explanations.

Proverbs 10:4 "Lazy hands bring poverty, but hard-working hands lead to wealth." Being financially responsible is a part of not being lazy. Racking up debt with no true intentions of paying it back, is a form of laziness that will soon lead you to poverty. When you become financial responsible, paying your debts, saving, and investing, will lead to wealth. Laziness all together will surely bring you to poverty. When you are lazy and have no money then you will depend on other people to take care of you.

Mark 12:17 "And Jesus answering said unto them, Render to Caesar the things that are Caesar's, and to God the things that are God's. And they marveled at him." God loves a cheerful giver and he will bless you more than you can imagine. Jesus also talks about what is owed to Caesar. You cannot live in this land and not pay taxes and pay your debts because that is foolish and will lead you to financial destruction. Not paying your debts will cause you to lose everything that you do have.

1 Timothy 5:8 "But if any provide not for his own, and

especially for those of his own house, he hath denied the faith, and is worse than an infidel." When you have gotten so far into debt that you cannot provide for your family you have a problem. You must gain control of the finances in your household. God has provided you with honest ways to provide. Do what you have to do to make an honest income. You might not be working the job that you want but continue to work and provide, keep the faith and God will provide the increase.

Proverbs 13:22 "A good man leaveth an inheritance to his children's children: and the wealth of the sinner is laid up for the just." The 60/40 rule will allow you to leave an inheritance to your children. When you leave this earth, you do not want to leave your children your debt, you want to leave your children generational wealth. Your freedom investing and long-term savings will allow you to leave a business or a home to your heirs. You should even invest in a life insurance plan to pay for end of life funeral costs.

Proverbs 21:5 "The thoughts of the diligent tend only to plenteousness; but of every one that is hasty only to want." Careful planning leads to profit. Acting too swiftly leads to poverty.

Consider those who rob and steal to gain wealth. Even those who shed blood for money. I rest my case.

For many people there is a mentality that clothes have value. They will go all out and spend a lot of money on clothes and sneakers. Clothes and sneakers have no value. A pair of sneakers costs around $10 to $15 a pair to make. They are usually made in foreign countries in sweat shops where workers are paid very low wages. A sneaker company can take $10,000 overseas and bring back a boat load of sneakers. Now, the mark up on sneakers is 1000%. There is nothing wrong with wanting nice things but you need to understand the value of what you are buying. The same shoes that people call knock offs are actually not knock offs. The same shoe that you paid $200 for is in Walmart, and family dollar without the logo. The sneaker was made in the same country by the same workers. You are not paying for the sneaker, you are paying for the logo that is on it. This is a question everybody must ask themselves. If what I buy, in terms of clothes and sneakers, really cost what I paid for them, why do clothes and sneakers go on sale and on clearance? Good question. The reason being is companies have wiggle room in the price of the product. Even if a $200 sneaker goes on sale for $180, the company is still making a profit. If you have to have expensive things then you really need to follow the 60/40 because it will allow you to have play money.

Here is another way to save. It is easy and simple to use. This is a savings plan that is spread out over 52 weeks. This was created on a Facebook group by a personal finance enthusiast Kassonda Perry-Moreland.

52 Week Money Challenge Saving Plan

week	Amount Deposited	Account Balance	Week	Amount Deposited	Account Balance
1	$1.00	$1.00	27	$27.00	$378.00
2	$2.00	$3.00	28	$28.00	$406.00
3	$3.00	$6.00	29	$29.00	$435.00
4	$4.00	$10.00	30	$30.00	$465.00
5	$5.00	$15.00	31	$31.00	$496.00
6	$6.00	$21.00	32	$32.00	$528.00
7	$7.00	$28.00	33	$33.00	$561.00
8	$8.00	$36.00	34	$34.00	$595.00
9	$9.00	$45.00	35	$35.00	$630.00
10	$10.00	$55.00	36	$36.00	$666.00
11	$11.00	$66.00	37	$37.00	$703.00
12	$12.00	$78.00	38	$38.00	$741.00
13	$13.00	$91.00	39	$39.00	$780.00
14	$14.00	$105.00	40	$40.00	$820.00
15	$15.00	$120.00	41	$41.00	$861.00
16	$16.00	$136.00	42	$42.00	$903.00
17	$17.00	$153.00	43	$43.00	$946.00
18	$18.00	$171.00	44	$44.00	$990.00
19	$19.00	$190.00	45	$45.00	$1,035.00
20	$20.00	$210.00	46	$46.00	$1,081.00
21	$21.00	$231.00	47	$47.00	$1,128.00
22	$22.00	$253.00	48	$48.00	$1,176.00
23	$23.00	$276.00	49	$49.00	$1,225.00
24	$24.00	$300.00	50	$50.00	$1,275.00
25	$25.00	$325.00	51	$51.00	$1,326.00
26	$26.00	$351.00	52	$52.00	$1,378.00

www.buildingourstory.com

As you can see you are only starting week one off with one dollar. Week two you add two dollars and have a balance of $3. If you struggle with saving definitely take a look at this.

Here are a few more things that will help you gain control of your finances.

-Live within your wages

Do not spend more than what you make. This may cause you to put your credit cards away. Too many people fall back to living off of credit when they are in financial distress. People who live off of a cash base spend 20 percent less and will not feel like they are getting robbed. They will not spend frivolously.

-Get in financial shape

Sometimes people will get so far in debt they will neglect paying their bills on time. They will not check their bank balance and their credit card statements. These types of habits will always ruin your credit. Always keep track of your bills.

-Don't overdraft your bank account

Check your balance daily. Most banks will send a daily text message with your account balance. Regularly check your account balance and transactions to ensure you do not overdraft your

account.

-Improve your credit

You can get a free copy of your credit report form

www.annualcreditreport.com. Review your credit report

thoroughly to see the damage(s) done. Contact creditors to work

out plans for repayment. If you are not comfortable contact a credit

or Debt specialist to help set up a plan for you.

Chapter 4 Reflections

How do you feel about you financial state? Would you be willing to try the 52 week savings challenge, if you haven't already?

_____

_____

_____

_____

_____

_____

_____

_____

_____

_____

_____

"It all belongs to God. You reap what you sow"

-Dr. Freddie E. Terry, Jr.

5 The Truth About Debt

Proverbs 22:7 "The rich ruleth over the poor, and the borrower is servant to the lender."

When you do a Google search on the definition of debt. It gives the definition of something, typically money, that is owed or due. When you owe something or when something is due, it has transitioned to a responsibility. God does not want us to be financial slaves.

This why Proverbs 22:7 is so important. Some people are working two and three jobs just to pay back their debts. They are slaves to the rich. This is not the life God wants for you.

Deuteronomy 15:6 For the LORD thy God blesseth thee, as he promised thee: and thou shalt lend unto many nations, but thou shalt not borrow; and thou shalt reign over many nations, but they shall not reign over thee. Be the lender and not the borrower. Break the chains of financial slavery that holds you back from what has been promised by God.

Proverbs 37:21 The wicked borroweth, and payeth not again: but the righteous sheweth mercy, and giveth. Do not be this person, do not borrow knowing that you cannot or will not pay it back.

How to get out of debt The truth is pay your bills on time and do not bite off more than you can chew. If you have bitten off more than you can chew do not worry because you can get out of debt. Some people want to get out of debt really fast, they want to play the lotto or wish for a lump sum of money. That is not reality. It took you some time to get into debt so it will take a little time to get out of it, which will be explained in great detail.

I learned the snowball effect from Dave Ramsey who is the author of "The Total Money Makeover". It works by lining up your debts from least to greatest. Do not worry about interest rates. Pay the minimum due to all of them. If you can add whatever extra you have to the smallest one. The reason being is so when you pay off the smallest one you can feel a sense of accomplishment. Then you take the minimum from that one plus the extra that you were paying to it and snowball it into the next bill. Each time you do that and pay your bills off, your snowball is getting bigger and gaining momentum to pay off your debts and knocking out one bill at a time. Think about how quickly you will be debt free. You are taking payments from a previous debt and rolling it into the next debt until it is paid off. When you pay the smallest bill off, go ahead a celebrate and mark that one off of your list.

Now some people are so stretched thin financially they cannot afford to pay the minimum to the rest of their bills. Then you just have to take one bill at a time until you can do so. In this process you cannot be overly concerned about your credit score. The reason being is because over time it will increase anyway as long as you are not making new debts. I can tell you this, in due season your credit situation will change, typically in 7 years. This is not saying not to pay your bills or pay off your credit but there is a passage in the bible that everyone needs to be made aware of. The Lord's Release is found in Deuteronomy 15:1-2. "At the end of every seven years thou shalt make a release. And this is the manner of the release: Every creditor that lendeth ought unto his neighbor shall release it; he shall not exact it of his neighbor, or of his brother; because it is called the LORD'S release." Many people over look this passage. God's word is true because if you look at it, there is no irony. The 7th year of your debt you are release from it. Your creditor shall not exact it of you. Which over time you will get offers in the mail with creditors willing to settle as time goes on.

Credit & credit cards: Here is where many people get suckered into debt. Especially young college students. Credit card companies prey on these young individuals knowing they need money but they have little income. If they have not received prior knowledge about credit cards and debt from their high school or parents they can be easily seduced. I have shared the system which helps you to set up that source. Before you know it, you can easily end up with $20,000 of credit card debt. It is best to have slowly built a $20,000 account than to borrow it and cannot pay it back. Credit Cards can be used to help you establish credit. If you cannot pay it off in 30 days do not charge it. Typically, you can use it for gas, groceries and then at the end of the month pay it off. You don't want to have a lot of revolving debt because it impacts your credit score a great deal. Every 90 days or so you can call your credit card company and negotiate your rates and your credit limits. Follow the script below and you cannot go wrong. Just so you know, when they talk to you they are reading from a script.

<u>Step One: Increasing Lines Of Credit</u>

Credit Card Script by Feridon Terry

You: Hello, I'm calling to make some adjustments to my current credit card. First, what is my current credit limit?

Operator: Hello, Your current limit is $_____

You: I am going to be making an important purchase and rather than using multiple cards, I would like to use this as my primary credit card. In order to do so, I will need to increase my limit.

Operator: How much would you like to increase?_____

You: How much will the system allow me to increase to? (if they offer less than you are looking for, continue to negotiate through steps two and three, then, ask to speak to a supervisor,

51

outlined in step four).

or

I would like my limit raised to $_____

Operator: The system will allow me to raise your limit to $_____ (If acceptable move on to step two)

Or

We will be back in touch with you in 72 hours, etc.,

You: What can you do for me today?

If it is not acceptable to you :

You: Thank you for your help, I would like to speak to your supervisor. (start from the beginning).

Step 2: Decreasing Interest Rates

You: What interest rate am I currently paying?

Operator:_____

You: I would like that lowered immediately

If they do not lowered the rate to your satisfaction:

You: I'm confused, I receive offers frequently that are for

_____%. I do realize a lot of those of introductory rates, but in

order for me to be more comfortable using this card as my primary

card, I would like for you to be more competitive. Can you

consider me at least part of the way for a limited time?

Operator: We can go down to _____ for _____

months.

Step 3: Eliminating Annual Fees

You: Am I currently paying an annual fee on this card?

Operator: You are pay $_____ per year

Student: What benefits do I receive for this fee?

Operator: You are receiving _____

(If you are paying just for privilege of holding the card).

You: I would like to have that credited and discontinued.

Operator: ok

The biggest mistake people make is ignoring the bill collectors calls. If you owe the debt, do your best to pay it back. I know some people who have lost their jobs, etc. It is difficult to pay your bills. It is better to answer the call and letting the bill collectors know that you are unemployed than to just ignore them altogether. Some creditors will put you in a hardship program that will not hurt you as bad as it going into collections or better yet, the creditor taking a judgement out against you. Most creditors will work around your budget when you are in financial distress. If you can try to pay something until you get back on your feet. Judgements are headaches and often times a headache to fix on your credit report as well. A judgement is when you have failed to pay a creditor and they take you to civil court. When this happens you need to make some type of payment arrangements or they will garnish your wages. Always attend your court dates for judgments or your paychecks will be looking slim until the debt is paid in full. After the judgment is paid in full always check your credit report to ensure that it has a zero balance and states, satisfied. You get one free credit report a year at www.annualcreditreport.com. It is a good idea to pull it every year because you may have some things on there that you are not aware of that could be hurting your score. Anything between 700 to 799 is consider good credit. Anything 800 to 830 is consider excellent credit. Anything below a 600 is poor credit. To have good to excellent credit you must pay your bills and pay them on time. Do not max out your credit cards. Do not have a lot of debt with huge balances on them.

Did you know that African Americans have 1.1 trillion spending power? We spend most of that in electronics, groceries, utilities and footwear. To really blow your mind, we spend a lot less for health care and pensions.

Chapter 5 Reflections

Debt can be devastating, but it is not the end of your world. Give

one example on how you can dissolve your debt.

_____

_____

_____

_____

_____

_____

_____

"You cannot be in debt and win." – Dave Ramsey

6 Entrepreneurship

Proverbs 12:1 "Whoso loveth instruction loveth knowledge: but he that hateth reproof is brutish."

There are a few definitions for entrepreneurship but they all have the same meaning. It is just having the ability to start a business and or growing a business. Why is Entrepreneurship so important? It is important because Entrepreneurs help keep the economy going. People are lead to believe that it costs a lot of money to start a business. Yes, you need to have some capital to obtain product, rent, office furniture, etc, but to actually incorporate it only costs $125. That is right, $125 dollars and you can call yourself CEO. Legalzoom.com will definitely assist you with that. Corporate lawyers will charge you thousands of dollars for this procedure. Legalzoom.com will charge $125 and will also fill out your articles of corporation paperwork. What are you waiting for? Go ahead and start that business that you always wanted!

Most people who want to start a business do not know where to find funding for a startup. Some people may be faced with credit challenges. Do not let that keep you from moving forward with your business. Google is your friend. There are many types of grants out there for your business. There are grants for women, black business owners, young entrepreneurs, and much more. What you have to understand about grants is, they are non-repayable. Meaning you do not have to pay that grant money back. Keep in mind though, you have to follow the guidelines that are outlined for the grant

Here is the link to the small business grant. https://www.sba.gov/blogs/government-grants-small-business-think-you-qualify

You may be the individual who wants to start a business but you do not know what kind of business. Keep this in mind when you are thinking about starting a business. "Take what you like and make that your hobby, take what other people like and make that your business." – Warren Buffett

Most people do not often start out as entrepreneurs. They may become one after working and gaining work experience then decide to start a business. Leaving your current full time job is risky. You will be leaving income that if you work you will get paid. Trading hours for wages is what I like to call it. If your business collapse, you will not have any income.

After you have incorporated your business you then need to obtain your EIN number. EIN stands for Employer Identification number. In other words, this is your business social security number. This number will help you establish business credit. You will be able to buy cars, houses, etc. in your business name. Now, this EIN number works just like your credit. Paying your bills is a must. If you have ever looked at your W-2s when you have filed taxes it has a EIN number at the top. You can have people work for you as well with this number. You can obtain it free at IRS.gov. It only takes about 5 to 10 minutes to fill out. You will get it back immediately as well as a letter in the mail with your official EIN number. I do not recommend you to do your own taxes. I do not recommend you to have a non-certified person to do your taxes. I do recommend that you seek a certified public account. They are very familiar with the tax laws.

If you are running a business and you have a store front you will need a business license to operate in that building. Typically they are obtained at the courthouse in the area you are operating. If not, they will direct you in the right location to get your business license.

A lot of people turn their noses up at network marketing businesses. It is because they have been programmed to believe that they are illegal. A pyramid structure is not a scheme. As a matter of fact the government, school systems and even your job uses this structure because it is the strongest structure. They call it the chain of command. For example, the POTUS sits on top, then Vice President, etc. Now there is a such thing called a pyramid scheme, this is without a doubt illegal. A pyramid scheme is when money is being exchange without any product or services being rendered. So if you are in a network marking company and it has a product or offers a service you are safe. Network marketing can be a good tool to get the money you need for your goals or a business that you want to start.

Real Estate – There is a hymnal "my father is rich in houses and land".

Real Estate defines as property consisting of land or buildings.

Real estate is one of the most secure ways to obtain wealth. No matter what people or experts say about the real estate market, people still need roofs over their heads. When you own houses and people are renting from you, you create what is called residual income. Residual income is income that continues to be generated after the initial effort has been expended. Compare this to what most people focus on earning: linear income, which is "one-shot" compensation or payment in the form of a fee, wage, commission or salary. Residual income the work is done one time and you get paid over and over. If you have a tenant and the tenant signs a lease, that work is done and the 1st of the month you have a check. The problem with linear income is if you do not show up for work you do not get paid. It is trading hours for wages. There are many other ways to make money in real estate. Most people focus on buying and holding. There is a such thing that is called wholesaling. Real estate wholesaling is similar to flipping except that the time frame is much shorter and no repairs are made to the home before the wholesaler sells it. A real estate wholesaler does a contract with the seller, markets the home to his potential buyers, and then assigns the contract to the buyer. You find distressed properties and motivated sellers. How you get them to contact you is putting up signs "we buy houses cash". I know you are thinking, where do I get the cash from? In the case of wholesaling, you do not need the cash yourself. You need to find the people with the cash that want to buy those kind of properties.

Chapter 6 Reflections

How much does it cost to start your own business?

_____

'Entrepreneur' denotes that you recognize that you are doing

things across disciplines and that you are blazing your own path.

–Pharrell Williams

7 The Power of The Mind

Romans 12: 2 "Do not be conformed to this world, but be transformed by the renewal of your mind, that by testing you may discern what is the will of God, what is good and acceptable and perfect."

Your mind is where everything starts. You use it for your everyday functions such as movement, speaking and walking. You possess thinking power. Some people *react* and then *think*, when they should *think* then *react*. The brain is a powerful muscle that is connected to a higher power, which is God. With that being said, there is nothing you can't do. You can do anything if you just put your mind to it. Your mind gives you the ability to create, generate and bring dreams to life.

When people were children, they dreamed all the time. They dreamed of playing a professional sport, being a doctor or lawyer. Somewhere between their childhood and adulthood they stopped dreaming. I challenge you to start dreaming again. Dreams lead to ideas, ideas lead to wealth.

I met one of my mentors, Bryant Stith a former NBA player, over 20 plus years ago. He gave me his autograph on a piece of paper. It read "Dream Big!" That stood out to me for more than 20 years and it solidified the notion that it is ok to have big goals and dreams. Don't cut yourself short of what you deserve.

People often times fall short of the dreams because they spend most of their time valuing other people's opinions. They keep listening to people who are broke, who are quitters, who are not about anything worth listening too. If you choose listen to these people, and their opinions, you will buy into their lifestyle.

Keep your mind sharp always. It needs exercise and the way you do that is through reading. Just as you are reading this book, reading will help open up your mind. Books are like pencil sharpeners. Just like pencils, if you never sharpen them the lead will eventually become dull.

"When I was a child, I spake as a child, I understood as a child, I thought as a child: but when I became a man, I put away childish things"1 Corinthians 13:11. It is nothing wrong with being a child.

There is something wrong with being an adult with a childlike mentality. You have to make up in your mind that it is time to move forward, grow up and let your mind and imagination take you to where you want to go.

Do not spend all of your life working on someone else's dreams and not your own. Imagination is the faculty or action of forming new ideas, or images or concepts of external objects not present to the senses according to google. As a kid growing up you probably have let your imagination run wild on several different occasions. You probably had dreams of going to the NBA, being an actress, or being a doctor. You might have even pretended to live out these dreams. As you became an adult, you stopped having an imagination. You were always told to have a backup plan when you were younger, just in case your real plan doesn't pan out. There is nothing wrong with having a backup plan. The problem is that so much effort went into the backup plan, that it became the original plan. In order for your dreams to come to fruition, you must give it your all.

A positive mind is a healthy mind. No matter what you are

faced with in life, remain positive. This will trigger your mind to find solutions to the problems you are faced with. For example, you need $500 for a set of tires. You don't have any extra money to buy a new set of tires. If you panic or have negative thoughts, you will shut your mind down. It will not trigger any thoughts on how to get or earn the money. A positive mind will go to work right away. Ideas will start to generate on how to get $500 dollars for the tires. You are in control of your mind. Your brain and tongue are the most powerful organs you have. Change your thinking, change your life.

Here are three things that will help you to control the power of the mind.

-Control your thoughts

Your mind sometimes can run away from you. The key to success is developing a winning mentality. When you unlock the power of the mind, you unlock a life with no limitations. What you think, is what you will become.

-Filter negative thoughts

Negative thoughts are poison to your potential and your abilities. These thoughts must be dissolved from the mind.

-Sow seeds of positive thoughts

What you sow is what you will reap. In order to sow positive thoughts, you have to be in the right place mentally. You have to change habits, old mindsets and old ways of thinking. In order for these things to take place you have to challenge your belief system.

Chapter 7 Reflections

Why is it important to keep your mind sharp?

_____

_____

_____

_____

_____

_____

_____

_____

_____

_____

"Your mind will always believe everything you tell it. Feed it faith. Feed it truth. Feed it with love."

-Unknown

8 Vision

Proverbs 29:18 "Where there is no vision, the people perish: but he that keepeth the law, happy is he"

If you research the definition of vision, it will state that vision is the faculty or state of being able to see. You do not need to have physical eye sight to have vision. Ray Charles had vision and he was a blind man. He envisioned how he wanted his music to sound. Although he was blind he had enough vision to take him where he wanted to go. Sound became his new set of eyes.

When you have no vision at all you will find yourself repeating the same cycles over and over. People will stay on the same jobs that they do not like. Hang around the same people who do not really want them to succeed. When you lack vision, you are somewhat blind.

One might ask, "how do I develop the ability to have vision?" First you must humble yourself and ask God to order your steps. God is the source, and his hotline is just a prayer away. I pray every day. I pray all day and I spend time with the Father. Sometimes when you sit in silence, God will show you things that you will need to know and do. I had to learn that after I realized my dreams of playing in the NBA started to wither away. I begin showing interest in real estate. My father was preaching and he said something that I still haven't forgotten till this day. "My father is rich in houses and land". This was a sign from God. I heard that and it stuck to me like glue. That was something that I wanted to do. I wanted to invest in real estate properties. I knew that by doing so, it would open the door to many other opportunities. I had some learning to do. I took courses, I asked for advice from others who were in the business and I developed relationships with many companies. God gave me a sign and I stuck to my vision.

It is very easy to lose sight of your vision. Your friends and sometimes your family will tell you that you can't do something or will tell you that it will not work. Sometimes you have to protect your vision. You have to guard it with your life. Everybody will not believe in your vision. That is because they cannot see it the way that you do. Often times the people around you will fear that your vision will come to culmination. They fear that you will be successful. Do not let that lead you astray. Even when you are sinking in the sand you must keep site of your vision. Soon as you look down your vision will become difficult to grasp. You will not sink in the sand. As a matter of fact, your focus and your drive will lift you above the sand and soar over it like an eagle.

Learning new things is always essential to the brain. It helps the mind focus on the pathways to birthing a vision. Having a vision is one of the most important elements in one's path to success. It helps defines the goal(s) ahead.

The more clear and precise the vision is the easier it will manifest itself to become a reality. Vision gives you the ability to see beyond your current circumstances. No matter what is taking place around you a vision is the reminder of why you are doing what you are doing. It helps you to keep that grit when you are being punished by adversity.

Develop a mental picture in your mind. Picture in your mind your desires and what steps that you need to take to get there.

Vision demands discipline and perseverance. Developing a vision is not difficult as long as you know what you want out of life.

Here are 14 scriptures that will help you with your God given vision. Bernard Haynes "Lead to Impact" came up with these very helpful scriptures.

1. Even though I walk through the valley of the shadow of death, I fear no evil for You are with me; Your rod and Your staff they comfort me. Psalm 23: 4

2. Trust in the LORD with all your heart and do not lean on your own understanding. In all your ways acknowledge Him and He will make your paths straight. Proverbs 3:5-6

3. Think on whatever is true, whatever is honorable, whatever is right, whatever is pure, whatever is lovely, whatever is of good repute, if there is any excellence and if anything worthy of praise,

dwell on these things. Philippians 4:712

4. Delight yourself in the Lord and He will give you the desires of your heart. Commit your way to the Lord, trust also in Him and He will do it. Psalm 37:4-5

5. Now to Him who is able to do far more abundantly beyond all that we ask or think, according to the power that works within us. Ephesians 5:201

6. This is the confidence which we have before Him that if we ask anything according to His will, He hears us. And if we know that He hears us in whatever we ask, we know that we have the requests which we have asked from Him. I John 5:14-15

7. If you abide in Me and My words abide in you, ask whatever you wish and it will be done for you. John 15:7

8. Be anxious for nothing, but in everything by prayer and supplication with thanksgiving let your requests be made known to God. And the peace of God, which surpasses all comprehension will guard your hearts and your minds in Christ Jesus. Philippians 4:6-7

9. Brethren, I do not regard myself as having laid hold of it yet; but one thing I do: forgetting what lies behind and reaching forward to what lies ahead. I press on toward the goal for the prize of the upward call of God in Christ Jesus. Philippians 3:13-14

10. For God has not given us a spirit of fear, but of power, love and sound mind. I Timothy 1:7

11. A good man leaves an inheritance to his children's children and the wealth of the sinner is stored up for the righteous. Proverbs 13:22

12. I can do all things through Him who strengthens me. Philippians 4:13

13. ...Have faith in God. Truly I say to you, whoever says to this mountain, be taken up and cast into the sea and does not doubt in his heart, but believes that what he says is going to happen, it will be granted him. Therefore I say to you, all things for which you pray and ask, believe that you have received them, and they will be granted you. Mark 5:22-24

14. Now faith is the substance of things hoped for, the evidence of things not seen. Hebrews 11:1

Chapter 8 Reflections

Why is having a vision so important?

_____

_____

_____

_____

_____

_____

_____

_____

_____

_____

_____

_____

_____

_____

_____

_____

_____

"Create the highest, grandest vision possible for your life,

because you become what you believe" –Oprah Winfrey

9 An Effective Leader

Matthew 7:12 "Therefore all things whatsoever ye would that men should do to you, do ye even so to them: for this is the law and the prophets.

A world leader is a person who leads or commands a group, organization, or country. Many people want to be in leadership roles but most of them fail miserably because they lack certain qualities of what a good leader possesses.

Effective leaders will frequently evaluate their strengths and weaknesses. Understanding your areas of weakness is setting yourself up for success. It is an opportunity for you to delegate to others those abilities to achieve whatever the common goal is. Effective leaders will have people around them who complement their flaws.

Effective leaders should be confident in what they do. People are naturally drawn to people with confidence. Being confident in their abilities to lead their people to what it is they are trying to accomplish. Being confident will allow you to not shy away from challenges or adversity.

Great leaders naturally communicate convincingly. They have a skill for divulging the right messages in the right moments. At all times they will attempt to deliver messages that inspire, motivate, reassure, and, when required, direct. This type of communication is the key to success.

Great leaders are considerate and have a good feel for the needs of their people. They understand what motivates their people and demonstrate sincere concern for their well-being. They want to understand what is going on with their people. This will always have people draw closer to you.

Great leaders see things through till the end. They always keep the main goal in their mind. They will eliminate anything they believe that is helping them achieve their goals. Giving up easy is not an option for them. It is not in their DNA.

Effective leaders are professional individuals. They are

conscience of their image, their actions and the way they communicate. They conduct themselves in a way that sets them apart from others. To differentiate yourself as an effective leader, you must lead by example. Be knowledgeable about your entire organization, and always speak intelligently.

Leaders take full responsibility for their people's performance and their own. When things are going in the right direction they give the appropriate recognition. When things require attention, they find ways to fix things quickly and get things back on track. When you can do this without singling out people for errors, or assigning blame to others to avoid taking responsibility yourself, you're being a responsible leader. This will take you far in leadership.

Passionate leaders seem to energize others easily, and they enthusiastically dive into most things with calculated caution. Your optimism, can liven up the workplace if it is genuine. Your subordinates moral is very important in effective leadership. If morale is low, it will be very difficult to get the best out of your people. Always look for ways to passionately stimulate and energize people and make work enjoyable and fun for you and your team. Great leaders are honest people and genuinely treat people how they like to be treated. They respect themselves and take others' feelings into consideration. .

Effective leaders are organizers and planners because they know it requires a thought process. Although thinking through various situations and possible impacts requires analytical thinking skills, plan so your passions align with your thinking. Lead with your heart and your head then victory will be yours.

I have had some really good leaders over the years. I have come across some who were very passionate about what they did and how they lead their employees. They took the time to get to know their personnel. I think that is very important when you are in a leadership role. If you do not take the time to learn some things about your personnel, how can you effectively help them to achieve the common goal?

Chapter 9 Reflections

What are some things that makes a leader effective?

_____

_____

_____

_____

_____

_____

_____

_____

_____

_____

"Ultimately, leadership is not about glorious crowning acts. It's about keeping your team focused on a goal and motivated to do their best to achieve it, especially when the stakes are high and the consequences really matter. It is about laying the groundwork for others' success, and then standing back and letting them shine."

-Chris Hadfield

10 Train Up Your Children

Proverbs 22:6 " Train up a child in the way he should go; and when is old, he will not depart from."

Children are like books with blank pages. It is up to us as parents to fill those pages. If not, the world will fill those pages and if you look closely, the world has absolutely lost its mine. The prince of air is going to and fro seeking whom he can destroy. The blank pages signifies the child's opportunity for training that will prepare them for life. When you start to fill those pages, you are training your child and building a strong foundation. Even when your child is led astray, they will return to that foundation.

Three things parents should not do.

1. Defend your child when he or she is wrong.
2. Saying yes all the time
3. Let the world raise your children

My father always told me growing up that if I was wrong he could not defend me. For a long time that baffled me. As I began to grow older it made much more sense. Defending your child when they are wrong opens a door that is filled with trouble. As a parent, when you defend your child when they are wrong it makes you look bad and your integrity is tarnished. You are making the statement to your child that they are invincible and free to do as they please. That is setting them up for failure. Some children will develop the habit of not respecting authority.

It is ok to tell your children no sometimes. Giving them everything they ask for is handicapping them. Let them earn some things. Some parents have a habit of rewarding bad behavior. When this occurs, the child can become out of control. Saying no sometimes will help your child become more appreciative in general. When things are given to them continuously they can become unappreciative.

Ever heard the saying "It takes a village to raise a child?" Now a days some parents do not want people saying anything to their children. Yes, you have to be mindful of who speaks to your child. In most instance, teachers, community leaders, and family are the people who, not raise YOUR children, but they are helping to raise them. Some parents do not want these individuals correcting their child. It is ok for a coach to be a little tough on your child. It is ok for a teacher wanting your child to succeed. If you spend most of your time trying to correct the people correcting your child, you will miss out on the opportunity to build a strong foundation for your child.

I highly recommend you to involve your child in sports and activities. Team sports teaches your child how to work with others. It will also help them to be more discipline. When I began to play sports, I learned how to be a leader. I became a motivator.

The reason you want to involve your kids in activities such as playing the piano, is because learning to use musical instruments will help your child develop mentally. You want to keep their young minds stimulated. If you cannot afford activities for your child, always check with your schools. Many schools have after school programs and summer camps.

Reading is a key that will open many doors to your child's future. Reading 30 minutes a day will help them build intellect.

Reading will also help your child pass any standardized test because it helps them develop comprehension. After your child reads, it is a good practice to allow your child to tell you what they read. This will allow you to see if your child understands what they are reading.

Know what your children are into. Technology is good for a lot of things. First, explain to your child what internet safety is about. In older days, parents could somewhat shield their children from the world. The world is now at the palm of their hands when you give them technology freely. Internet safety is just teaching your child to use the internet and technology responsibly. Technology is the way of the world. Your children use it daily at school. It has helped many of them learn in numerous ways. Some parents may not understand their child's homework but with a few clicks using the internet, parents can understand a little better.

Did you know?

Between the ages of 2 and 5 a child develops in these main areas;

physical development, cognitive development, emotional and

social development, language, sensory and motor development

"God put us here to prepare this place for the next generation. That's our job. Raising children and helping the community, that's preparing for the next generation."

-Dikembe Mutombo

11 Born To Win

Romans 8:28 "And we know that all things work together for good to them that love God, to them who are the called according to his purpose."

With this knowledge that you know you possess, you better understand why you are born to win. You have to have the courage to stand on what you believe. Courage to keep moving forward no matter what you are faced with. You have to stop fearing the unknown because there is nothing to fear but fear itself. You were created in God's image and his likeness so therefore believe that there is nothing that can stop you.

Don't let the fear of failure control your life. Don't think that you are completely done because you have lost a few battles. You may have lost a few but the war is far from over. Take on the warrior mentality and refuse defeat, refuse to lose because you know that you were born to win. No that failure is just a log to remind you how you got to where you are. It is a blueprint to give others so that they may be guided in their battles. Your blueprint can help others win their wars.

Remember everyone that is around you may not be for you. Some of them do not even realize they could be hindering you from your greatness. It is imperative to check your circle to see where the mindsets are. If they are not trying to build and grow with you, they are not for you. You have to make a decision. Either you want to achieve and reach your destiny or continue to entertain people who want to remain stagnant. You are what you believe. You are who you associate yourself with.

Remember to take care of your finances so that you can be blessed. Be a good steward over what you have so that you can blessed to have more. Learn to budget your money so that you do not spend what you do not have. Do not be foolish and splurge because you want to impress people. That is the fastest way that you can get in debt. Yet, take care of your priorities. Look to leave something behind for the generation behind you.

Debt can have you in financial slavery. Working just to pay your bills. Remember, companies make their money banking of you being in debt. Take care of your credit, and save for the things that you want. If you find yourself drowning in debt, it is not over. God does not want you live your life in that way. He wants you to live life in abundance. It is hard to do that when lenders have shackles on your hands and feet. You can break those chains but you must first know that it took you time to get in debt and it will take a little time to get out of it.

The first I ever heard about entrepreneurship I was around the young age of 18. I always wondered how people owned businesses. How they had people working for them. I begin to study entrepreneurship and found that if I wanted to own things it would not come from a job alone. Entrepreneurship in most instances can free you from a regular 9 to 5. There is no cap on the amount of income you can make by being an entrepreneur. You have to be willing to take risks. You have to be willing to sacrifice things such as time to put towards your goals in your business or ventures as an entrepreneur. Seek out mentors, people who are in the same field as you. Learn to build relationships in the world of entrepreneurship. It can help you reach your ultimate goal as an entrepreneur.

Your mind is powerful. It is important to keep it sharp. Feed it with knowledge that will help you in life. What you think, you will become. I think that I am great, therefore I will become great. Greatness is what I will attract. The things that you want to do in life first starts in the mind. It is the laboratory where things are created. You must be careful of what you put in your body because it could ultimately have an effect on your mind. You do not want to have a cloudy mind.

A cloudy mind can affect your vision. Vision is very important. You have to see what it is your want out of life. You have to see where you are going. When you lack vision, you can become stationary. You can become blind in a sense. It is imperative your vision is clear and precise. Your vision will help you set your goals and help you keep your eyes on the prize.

When people get in leadership roles they believe they have to be this horrible dictator and make people's lives miserable in order to get things done. Respect is earned and when you give it, you will get it in return. Learn who works for you, learn their strengths

and weaknesses so that they can help you achieve the common

goal. Communication is the key in being effective as a leader. It's

ok to tell your staff or subordinates that they are doing a good job.

They need to hear that to help build their moral. As a leader you

can make them feel like they make a difference, that they are

valued. If you treat them as if they are easily replaced, they will

not go above and beyond for you.

Teach your children and help them grow into productive

citizens. Remember that they are open books with blank pages and

you have to make the decision that you will fill them or let the

world fill those pages. Teach them the right things to do in life.

Teach them love and respect for others. You cannot be your child's

friend, you have to be their parent. It's ok to tell them no from time

to time because in the long run, it will save their life.

I cannot stress enough about doing what's right. Keep that in

mind, doing the right thing in life. Even when the world thinks it is

not popular but doing what's right will eventually pay off. When

you know something is wrong, stand against it and do not justify something that is wrong. Doing the right thing will always give you a peace of mind.

Just live, you cannot worry about what others think, you cannot worry about what you do not have. Live in the moment, live for your children, your family, your loved ones. Life is a gift from the most high being in our universe. It is worth more than any goods in the world, because it is not manmade. The breath of life, that many take for granted. You are rich because of it. I challenge you to live.

I challenge everyone to find the positive in every negative situation that you are faced with. Photographers, before digital photography, use to take negatives and put them in a solution to get positive pictures. You have to take the negative and find the solution so your outcome can become positive. Find a way.

I challenge you when you fall - get back up again. I challenge you to keep going when people tell you that you should stop. People can't not see your vision the way that you do. I challenge you to set goals and have pathways to achieve them. I challenge you to help others in need. Give them knowledge that will help them on their journey. Be a light unto the world so that the ones in the dark may be driven to the light. No negativity is allowed and if it decides to show up, turn it around and drive it out. In the words of Walt Disney "KEEP MOVING FORWARD"

Born to Win

"I am the vine; you are the branches. The one who remains in me -
and I in him - bears much fruit, because apart from me you can
accomplish nothing." -John 15:5

"For the past 33 years, I have looked in the mirror every morning and asked myself: 'If today were the last day of my life, would I want to do what I am about to do today?' And whenever the answer has been 'no' for too many days in a row, I know I need to change something." - Steve Jobs

How do you feel about yourself after reading this book?

_____

_____

_____

_____

_____

_____

_____

_____

Feridon's Top 20 Vocabulary Words

1. Invest – expend money with the expectation of achieving a profit

2. IRA – individual retirement account allows individuals to direct pretax income towards

3. Stock – the goods or merchandise kept on the premises of a business or warehouse and available for sale.

4. CPA – certified public accountant is an accounting professional who has passed the uniform CPA exam and have met the state requirements.

5. Mutual Fund – the pooled money that is invested in assests.

6. Entrepreneur – a person who organizes and operates a business or businesses.

7. LLC – limited liability company is a business structure that combines the pass through taxation of a partnership with the limited liability of a company

8. APR – annual percentage rate is charged for borrowing funds.

9. Fixed APR – is the amount of interest charged for a loan or

credit card over a year.

10. Accounts payable – a debtor's accounts of money he owes.

11. Accounts receivable – a creditor's accounts of money owed to him.

12. Asset – a useful or valuable quality.

13. Bankruptcy – inability to discharge all your debts.

14. Capital – assets available for use in the production of further assets.

15. Certificate of deposit – a debt instrument issued by a bank, usually pays interest.

16. Debt – state of owing something , especially money.

17. Dividend – earnings of a corporation distributed to it's shareholders.

18. Investor – someone who commits capital to gain financial returns.

19. Money Market – a market for short term instruments.

20. Real estate – property consist of houses and land.

Resources to help

www.creditkarma.com

www.annualcreditreport.com

www.legalzoom.com

www.irs.gov

www.clearpointcredit.org

Cites:

Holy Bible, King James Version for scripture references

Ramsey, Dave. *The Total Money MakeOver*. Nashville, Nelson Books. 2003

Brainy Quotes for various quotes throughout the book, www.brainyquotes.com

Ellis, Blake. *40 Million Americans Have Student Loan Debt.* http://money.cnn.com/2014/09/10/pf/college/student-loans/ September 10, 2014.

Unknown. *35 percent of Americans Have Unpaid Debt.* www.huffingtonpost.com August 7, 2015

Perry-Moreland, Kassonda. *52 Week Savings Plan.* http://www.bankrate.com/finance/savings/take-52-week-money-challenge-1.aspx 2013.

Haynes, Bernard. Lead to Impact.

http://leadtoimpact.com/about-us-2/meet-bernard/

Economy, P. (2014, October 17). *http://www.inc.com/author/peter-economy*.

Kiyosaki, R. (2008, May). *Rich Dad Education*.

www.ingramcontent.com/pod-product-compliance
Lightning Source LLC
Chambersburg PA
CBHW051331170526
45166CB00002B/769